HAVE FUN READING THIS BOOK!

IT OFFERS SOME REAL SURVIVAL TIPS. BUT THE SETTINGS ARE NOT REAL. THINK ABOUT HOW YOU CAN USE THESE HACKS IN REAL LIFE. USE COMMON SENSE. BE SAFE AND ASK AN ADULT FOR PERMISSION AND HELP WHEN NEEDED.

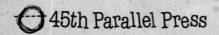

45th Parallel Press

Published in the United States of America by Cherry Lake Publishing
Ann Arbor, Michigan
www.cherrylakepublishing.com

Reading Adviser: Marla Conn, MS, Ed., Literacy specialist, Read-Ability, Inc.
Book Designer: Felicia Macheske

Photo Credits: By Malinovskaya Yulia/Shutterstock.com, cover; © Rick Partington/Shutterstock.com, 5;
© Monkey Business Images/Shutterstock.com, 6; © Sergey Nivens/Shutterstock.com, 9; © Khanumnaow/
Shutterstock.com, 11; © INDz/Shutterstock.com, 13; © alexandre zveiger/Shutterstock.com, 14; © Bohbeh/
Shutterstock.com, 17; © Nastyaofly/Shutterstock.com, 22; © graja/Shutterstock.com, 25; © Mariyana M/
Shutterstock.com, 27; © AlenKadr/Shutterstock.com, 29

Other Images Throughout: © SrsPvl Witch/Shutterstock.com; © Igor Vitkovskiy/Shutterstock.com; © FabrikaSimf/
Shutterstock.com; © bulbspark/Shutterstock.com; © donatas1205/Shutterstock.com; © NinaM/Shutterstock.
com; © Picsfive/Shutterstock.com; © prapann/Shutterstock.com; © S_Kuzmin/Shutterstock.com © autsawin
uttisin/Shutterstock.com; © xpixel/Shutterstock.com; © OoddySmile/Shutterstock.com; © ilikestudio/
Shutterstock.com; © Kues/Shutterstock.com; © ankomando/Shutterstock.com; © ctrlaplus/Shutterstock.com;
© popicon/Shutterstock.com; © Malinovskaya Yulia/Shutterstock.com; © Dshnrgc/Shutterstock.com

45th Parallel Press is an imprint of Cherry Lake Publishing.

Library of Congress Cataloging-in-Publication Data

Names: Loh-Hagan, Virginia, author.
Title: Lost in space hacks / by Virginia Loh-Hagan.
Description: Ann Arbor, MI : Cherry Lake Publishing, [2019] | Series: Could
 you survive? | Includes bibliographical
 references and index.
Identifiers: LCCN 2019006166| ISBN 9781534147836 (hardcover) | ISBN
 9781534150690 (pbk.) | ISBN 9781534149267 (pdf) | ISBN 9781534152120
 (hosted ebook)
Subjects: LCSH: Space vehicle accidents—Juvenile literature. | Space
 flight—Juvenile literature. | Survival—Juvenile literature. | Outer
 space—Juvenile literature.
Classification: LCC TL867 .L64 2019 | DDC 629.45—dc23
LC record available at https://lccn.loc.gov/2019006166

Cherry Lake Publishing would like to acknowledge the work of The Partnership for 21st Century Skills.
Please visit *www.p21.org* for more information.

Printed in the United States of America
Corporate Graphics

Dr. Virginia Loh-Hagan is an author, university professor, former classroom teacher, and curriculum designer.
She wrote a 45th Parallel Press book about *Apollo 13*. She lives in San Diego with her very tall husband and very
naughty dogs. To learn more about her, visit www.virginialoh.com.

COULD YOU SURVIVE

LOST
IN SPACE?

THIS BOOK COULD SAVE YOUR LIFE!

You could be trapped in outer space. Outer space is the vast area that exists beyond Earth. It exists between space objects. Space objects include stars and planets.

You can't live in space. You need a spacesuit. You can only live in space shuttles or space labs. Outer space is empty space. It's a very **hostile** place. Hostile means unkind. There's no air. You can't breathe in outer space. Without air pressure, your blood would bubble. Your body would swell up. Your brain would shut down.

TIP Wear a spacesuit. Spacesuits hold air for people to breathe. They also protect against the sun's rays, heat, and cold.

There are other dangers in outer space. You could get hit by **asteroids**. Asteroids are small rocks that circle the sun. You could get hit by space junk. You could get hit by space dust. Things in space move at high speeds.

Outer space has extreme weather. The sun is really hot. It'd burn your skin. Space is also really cold. You'd freeze to death. In space, it can be difficult to move. You could lose control.

There are 3 choices for survival. First, get back to the space shuttle. Second, wait for rescue. Third, find a new planet.

TIP Be smart with what you pack. You can only use what you brought.

You may be lost in space. But hope is not lost. You might be one of the lucky survivors. You have to be smart. First, check out the tools you have. Second, remember your **astronaut** training. Astronauts are people who travel to space.

Most importantly, know how to survive. Keep this in mind:

- You can only live 3 minutes without air.

- You can only live 3 days without water.

- You can only live 3 weeks without food.

This book offers you survival **hacks**, or tricks. Always be prepared. Good luck to you.

TIP Work with NASA for any space travel.

SCIENCE CONNECTION

Space shuttles are amazing. They carry people and things to space. They need a lot of speed and energy to fight gravity. Gravity is a force. It pulls objects back to Earth. Space shuttles are made of 3 parts. The parts are orbiter, external fuel tank, and solid rocket boosters. Space shuttles launch like rockets. The orbiter and boosters help shuttles blast off. Boosters force space shuttles up from Earth's gravity. This force is called thrust. Boosters drop off 2 minutes after launch. They fall into the ocean. A special boat picks them up. Boosters are used for another flight. The tank holds gas. It drops off too. It burns up over Earth. This happens when the shuttle uses all the gas. The orbiter returns to Earth. It has wings and a tail. It lands like an airplane. It's also used for another flight. A typical space shuttle weighs around 200,000 pounds (90,718 kilograms). It would need 4 million pounds (2 million kg) of gas to launch.

CHAPTER 1

WORK OUT!

Oh no! You're stuck in the space shuttle. You've lost contact with Earth. But NASA prepared you. Wait to be saved. You need to exercise. Bodies in space lose bone density and muscle. Make exercise bands.

TIP Work out for 2.5 hours a day. Astronauts do this.

HACK

1. Get something that stretches. This could be pantyhose, bungee cords, or spandex.

2. Get **carabiners**. These are special links. They're metal loops.

3. Tie the stretchy material to the carabiners.

4. Wrap duct tape around 2 cardboard pieces. Tape around 2 carabiners. These will be your handles.

5. Stretch out to do arm exercises.

6. Cut out 2 cardboard pieces for your feet. Wrap with duct tape. Place in the center of the band. Step on them. Use to do leg exercises.

TIP Tether yourself to the shuttle. Tether means to strap.

The key to this hack is **elastic force**.

Elastic force is resistance. Something that's elastic stretches out. It can also be **compressed**. Compressed means to be made smaller. Elastic things can be returned to their original shape. They resist the change in shape.

Pulling on the band stretches it. But the band won't break. The farther you stretch, the greater the resistance. This resistance works out your muscles. Muscles tighten against the band. This builds strength.

Resistance training causes small tears to muscles. Bodies quickly fix the muscles. Muscles grow again. They grow stronger.

CHAPTER 2

LET THE BAND PLAY ON!

Work out your mind as well. It can be lonely in space. Don't lose your mind. Playing musical instruments is good for your brain. Make a **xylophone**. Xylophones make sounds when their bars are hit.

HACK

1. Get bars. This could be paper rolls, pipes, or wooden bars.

2. Cut the bars. Cut them at different lengths. Make the lengths 1 inch (2.5 centimeters) apart.

3. Take the first 2 smallest bars. Put a rubber band around 1 bar. Twist it to make a figure 8. Put the other loop around the next bar. Hold them in place.

4. Do this to all the bars.

5. Attach to the sides of a box.

6. Make 2 **mallets**. Mallets are like drumsticks. Ball up paper. Duct tape to a pencil top.

TIP Play games. Always be thinking.

STEM

The key to this hack is pitch.

Pitch is the quality of sound. It makes sounds high. Or it makes sounds low. Xylophone bars make pitches. The pitch of each bar is determined by its length. Longer bars have a lower pitch. Shorter bars have a higher pitch. Bars are arranged in the same way as a piano. The low notes are on the left. The high notes are on the right.

Pitch is also related to **frequency**. Frequency is how often a sound wave passes through a certain point. Pitch depends on frequency. High pitches have high frequency waves. Low pitches have low frequency waves.

TIP Play music. Sing along.

REAL-LIFE CONNECTION

Astronauts need spacesuits to live in space. Spacesuits are like a one-person spacecraft. They let astronauts bend and move. They store air and water. They have other useful tools. Cameron Smith is an anthropologist. Anthropologists study the history of humans. Smith teaches at Portland State University. He likes exploring. He dives. He climbs mountains. He's survived arctic winters in Iceland and Alaska. Now, he wants to explore space. He made his own spacesuit. He did this with his own money. His spacesuit costs a lot less than a NASA suit. (A NASA suit costs $12 million.) He plans on testing his spacesuit. He'll take it up in a hot air balloon. He'll go up to 50,000 feet (15 kilometers). This is higher than what planes fly. He said, "Most people start to realize it's a lot of work. I don't know of anyone else designing a spacesuit privately."

CHAPTER 3

GRAB THINGS!

Gravity acts differently in space. Gravity is a force. On Earth, it attracts all objects toward the Earth's center. In space, astronauts float. Make a tool that helps you grab things. Collect your tools for survival.

HACK

1. Ball up paper.

2. Wrap duct tape around it. This holds the ball together.

3. Use the sticky side of the tape. Wrap a top layer. The top layer should have the sticky side out.

4. Stick a pole in the ball. This is the handle.

5. Aim the ball at your object. Jam against the object to grab hold.

TIP Use Velcro. Astronauts use Velcro to grab things.

explained by
STEM

The key to this hack is adhesion.

Adhesion is the ability of surfaces to cling to one another. It's also known as stickiness.

Duct tape sticks because of 2 forces. One is **wetting**. Wetting is how well an adhesive sinks into materials. Duct tape sinks into surface **pores**. Pores are tiny holes.

The second force that causes duct tape to stick is **van der Waals**. Van der Waals forces are weak attractions between **molecules**. Molecules are the smallest units of objects. They might not normally attract. But duct tape molecules are carefully arranged. They form bonds with the object's molecules. They stick.

TIP Use duct tape to close up leaks.

CHAPTER 4

TEST THE SOIL!

If there's no rescue, look for a planet. You need a planet that has air and water. Once on it, grow food. Plant your own garden. But first, test the soil.

TIP Keep seeds from plants. This is so you can grow more.

HACK

1. Get a clear jar with a lid.

2. Fill it halfway with soil.

3. Fill the rest with water. Leave an inch for shaking.

4. Put the lid on the jar. Shake the jar. Do this for about 5 minutes.

5. Leave it alone for 1 day.

6. Look for 3 layers. The bottom is sand. It should be rocky. The middle layer is silt. The top layer is clay.

7. Test it. The soil should be 20 percent clay, 40 percent silt, and 40 percent sand. If not, add things to make it so.

TIP Plant herbs. Many herbs can be used for medicine.

STEM

The key to this hack is soil.

Soil is **organic** material. Organic means coming from nature or living things. Soil is at the Earth's surface. It changes over time. It's affected by weather. It's affected by life. It's affected by death.

Soil is important for plants. It holds **roots**. Roots support plants. They store **nutrients**. Nutrients are healthy substances. Roots take food and water from the soil. They send food and water to plants. Soil helps to balance water and air. Sand and silt let water drain. It lets air flow. Clay holds the plant.

SPOTLIGHT BIOGRAPHY

Ellison Shoji Onizuka lived from 1946 to 1986. He was the first Asian American astronaut in space. He was from Hawaii. He was an Eagle Scout. He studied aerospace engineering. He graduated from the University of Colorado at Boulder. He was in the U.S. Air Force. He was a flight test engineer. He was a test pilot. He had over 1,700 flight hours. He applied to be an astronaut. He was one of over 8,000 applicants. In 1978, he was chosen. He flew on the *Discovery*. He circled Earth 48 times. In 1986, he was assigned to the *Challenger*. There was a leak. The shuttle exploded 73 seconds after launch. Onizuka died. He was buried in Hawaii. He said, "Every generation has the obligation to free men's minds for a look at new worlds . . . to look out from a higher plateau than the last generation."

CHAPTER 5

MAKE WATER!

Hopefully, your new planet has drinking water. If not, make water. Make a **solar still**. Solar means sun. A still is a tool that cleans **liquids**. Liquids are water forms.

TIP Look for comets. Comets are bits of ice and rock. Top layers fall off. Ice is locked inside. It melts.

HACK

1. Dig a pit. Make it 4 feet (122 cm) wide. Make it 3 feet (91 cm) deep.

2. Dig another hole in the center. Place a water container in it. (If available, place leaves around the container.)

3. Cover the pit with a plastic sheet.

4. Put rocks at the corners.

5. Put small a rock in the center of the sheet. Put it just above the container. Push the rock down gently. The sheet should slope at a 45-degree angle.

6. Secure the edges. Add rocks and dirt.

7. Wait 1 to 2 days. Don't open. Don't let water escape.

TIP Protect your skin while in the sun.

STEM

The key to this hack is the sun.

Solar stills use the sun's energy. They make water. Sun hits the plastic. It brings heat. Air inside becomes full of water. It **condenses**. Condensation is the changing from gas to liquid. This process makes clean water. Water drops collect on the plastic. They roll down the slopes. They roll into the container.

Solar stills can also be made to clean water. You'll have to add more containers. Dirty water is placed inside. The sun heats the water. Water changes into **vapor**. Vapor is gas. Water **evaporates** into the plastic. Evaporation is the changing of liquids into gas. Clean water forms on the plastic.

DID YOU KNOW?

- Yuri Gagarin was a Russian. He was the first man in space. He went to space in 1961. His space flight lasted 108 minutes. He circled Earth. He came back a hero.

- Neil Armstrong and Buzz Aldrin were the first 2 humans on the moon. They were on *Apollo 11*. Armstrong took the first step on the moon. He said, "That's one small step for man, one giant leap for mankind." This was the first manned moon landing mission. Manned means flown by a human. This happened on July 20, 1969.

- *Apollo 13* was to be the third mission to the moon. Its goal was to bring back moon pieces. It lifted off on April 11, 1970. The crew heard a loud bang. They were worried. They thought the number 13 was unlucky. They thought *Apollo 13* would be unlucky. Also, the launch time was 1:13 p.m. This is 13:13 in military time. The astronauts were 4 days away from Earth. The shuttle lost power. It had leaks. But the crew survived. They returned home safely.

- Christa McAuliffe was a high school teacher. In 1984, President Reagan and NASA started the Teacher in Space Program. They wanted a teacher who could teach students while in space. She was the first civilian in the history of space flight. On January 28, 1986, she boarded the *Challenger*. Six other people went. Their shuttle exploded. McAuliffe died.

- The International Space Station (ISS) was launched in 1998. It's a research lab in space. It's also a base for space travelers. It's the largest structure humans put into space. Over 230 people from 18 countries have been to the ISS. Peggy Whitson is an American astronaut. She set records. She flew 3 missions to the ISS. She spent 665 days in space. She's walked in space for over 60 hours.

CONSIDER THIS!

TAKE A POSITION!

Would you rather be lost in space or trapped in an alien invasion? Argue your point with reasons and evidence.

SAY WHAT?

Learn about astronauts. Explain how they train for space travel. Explain how they live in space.

THINK ABOUT IT!

Outer space is huge. There's so much we don't know. Do you think there's life beyond Earth? Do you think there are aliens? Do you think we could live on other planets? If so, would you go? Why or why not?

LEARN MORE!

Anderson, Clayton, and Scott Brundage (illust.). *A Is for Astronaut.* Ann Arbor, MI: Sleeping Bear Press, 2018.

Loh-Hagan, Virginia. *Apollo 13: Mission to the Moon.* Ann Arbor, MI: 45th Parallel Press, 2018.

Tyson, Neil deGrasse. *StarTalk: Everything You Ever Need to Know About Space Travel, Sci-Fi, the Human Race, the Universe, and Beyond.* Washington, DC: National Geographic, 2016.

GLOSSARY

adhesion (ad-HEE-zhuhn) the ability of surfaces to cling to one another

asteroids (AS-tuh-roidz) small rocks that circle the sun

astronaut (AS-truh-nawt) a person who trains to travel in space

carabiners (kar-uh-BEEN-urz) metal loops used to link things

compressed (kuhm-PRESD) made smaller, packed or pulled in

condenses (kuhn-DENS-iz) changes from gas to liquid

elastic force (ih-LAS-tik FORS) resistance to changing shape

evaporates (ih-VAP-uh-rates) changes from liquid into gas

frequency (FREE-kwuhn-see) how often a sound wave passes through a certain point

gravity (GRAV-ih-tee) a force that attracts objects toward the Earth's center

hacks (HAKS) tricks

hostile (HAH-stuhl) unkind, harsh, brutal

liquids (LIK-widz) water forms

mallets (MAL-its) drumsticks

molecules (MAH-luh-kyoolz) groups of atoms bonded together representing the smallest unit of chemical compounds

nutrients (NOO-tree-uhnts) substances that provide nourishment needed for growth

organic (or-GAN-ik) coming from natural things

pitch (PICH) quality of sound

pores (PORZ) tiny holes on surfaces

roots (ROOTS) parts of plants that attach to the ground and carry food and water to the plants

solar still (SOH-lur STIL) a tool that makes or cleans water using the sun's energy

van der Waals (VAN DUR WALZ) a force that attracts molecules that have a weak attraction

vapor (VAY-pur) gas

wetting (WET-ing) the process in which an adhesive penetrates or sinks into a surface

xylophone (ZYE-luh-fone) a musical instrument that makes sounds when bars are hit by mallets

INDEX